Table of Contents

INTRODUCTION 4
CHAPTER ONE 5
What is CBD oil? 5
Is CBD marijuana? 21
Where does CBD come from? 22
How CBD works 22
Benefits 24
    Quitting smoking and drug withdrawals 25
    Epilepsy 26
    Risks 28
How to use 29
The Difference Between CBD and THC 32
How CBD Oil Makes You Feel 33
CBD Oil Serving Sizes & Safety 33
Harvesting and transport 34
What is Epidiolex? 37
Important Information 37
Before taking this medicine 38
How should I take Epidiolex? 39
Epidiolex Dosing Information 41

What happens if I miss a dose? 47

What happens if I overdose? 47

What should I avoid while taking Epidiolex? 47

What other drugs will affect Epidiolex? 48

What's the difference between Epidiolex and other CBD products? 49

Epidiolex 51

How Does the FDA Approval Process Work? 61

Take a closer look at the FDA approval process. 62

CHAPTER TWO 65

Dog Seizures: 65

What Causes Seizures in Dogs... 65

Seizures in Small Dogs 66

Seizures in Older Dogs 67

Can They Have Epileptic Seizures 68

A Scary Situation for Pet Owners 69

Symptoms of Seizures in Dogs 69

What To Watch Out For—Dog Seizure Symptoms 69

Types of Seizures in Dogs 71

Cluster Seizures in Dogs 71

Focal Seizures in Dogs 72

Idiopathic Epilepsy 72

- Psychomotor Seizure ... 73
- Can Dog Seizures Be Cured, Stopped, or Prevented? ... 74
- How to Stop a Dog Seizure ... 74
- Tips on how to Handle Dog Seizures ... 76
- Dog Seizure Medication ... 77
- Natural Remedies for Dog Seizures ... 79
  - What Are They? Can they work? ... 79
  - Dog Seizure Treatment Home Remedy ... 79
- How to Gain Seizure Control ... 81
- The Basics of Dog Seizures ... 81
  - An Effective Treatment Method ... 83
- How do you use CBD for dog seizures? ... 86
- Benefits Of Cannabis Oil For Dogs ... 87
- CBD Oil For Dog Seizures – How It Works? ... 90
- What Research Says? ... 92
- What Is The Accurate Dosage Of CBD Oil For Dogs? ... 94
  - How To Administer CBD Oil To The Dogs? ... 96
  - Potential Risks Of CBD Oil On Dogs ... 97
  - Best CBD Oil For Dogs ... 99
  - Verified Dog Treats of CBD ... 101
- CONCLUSION ... 103

INTRODUCTION

Did you know dogs can have seizures? If your pup has experienced recurrent canine seizures, chances are your veterinarian has discussed some of the more common methods of pharmaceutical treatment.

The usual suspects include diazepam, potassium bromide, and other anticonvulsant drugs. The problem is, the side effects of these drugs can be quite serious for our dogs. However, a new method of treatment is catching the eye of veterinarians nationwide – cannabidiol (CBD).

This BOOK will provide some basic information on CBD for dog seizures and discuss how CBD can be an effective treatment for dog seizures.

CHAPTER ONE

What *is* CBD oil?

Cannabidiol is a popular natural remedy used for many common ailments. Better known as CBD, it is one of over 100 chemical compounds known as cannabinoids found in the cannabis or marijuana plant, Cannabis sativa.

Tetrahydrocannabinol (THC) is the main psychoactive cannabinoid found in cannabis, and causes the sensation of getting "high" that's often associated with marijuana. However, unlike THC, CBD is not psychoactive.

This quality makes CBD an appealing option for those who are looking for relief from pain and other symptoms without the mind-altering effects of marijuana or certain pharmaceutical drugs.

CBD oil is made by extracting CBD from the cannabis plant, then diluting it with a carrier oil like coconut or hemp seed oil.

It's gaining momentum in the health and wellness world, with some scientific studies confirming it may ease symptoms of ailments like chronic pain and anxiety.

Here are seven health benefits of CBD oil that are backed by scientific evidence.

1. Can Relieve Pain

Marijuana has been used to treat pain as far back as 2900 B.C. More recently, scientists have discovered that certain components of marijuana, including CBD, are responsible for its pain-relieving effects.

The human body contains a specialized system called the endocannabinoid system (ECS), which is involved in regulating a variety of functions including sleep, appetite, pain and immune system response.

The body produces endocannabinoids, which are neurotransmitters that bind to cannabinoid receptors in your nervous system.

Studies have shown that CBD may help reduce chronic pain by impacting endocannabinoid receptor activity, reducing inflammation and interacting with neurotransmitters.

For example, one study in rats found that CBD injections reduced pain response to surgical incision, while another rat study found that oral CBD treatment significantly reduced sciatic nerve pain and inflammation (5Trusted Source, 6Trusted Source).

Several human studies have found that a combination of CBD and THC is effective in treating pain related to multiple sclerosis and arthritis.

An oral spray called Sativex, which is a combination of THC and CBD, is approved in several countries to treat pain related to multiple sclerosis.

One study of 47 people with multiple sclerosis examined the effects of taking Sativex for one month. The participants experienced improvements in pain, walking, and muscle spasms. Still, the study didn't include any control group and placebo effects cannot be ruled out.

Another study found that Sativex significantly improved pain during movement, pain at rest and sleep quality in 58 people with rheumatoid arthritis. CBD, especially in combination with THC, may be effective in reducing pain associated with diseases like multiple sclerosis and rheumatoid arthritis.

2. Could Reduce Anxiety and Depression

Anxiety and depression are common mental health disorders that can have devastating impacts on health and well-being.

According to the World Health Organization, depression is the single largest contributor to disability worldwide, while anxiety disorders are ranked sixth.

Anxiety and depression are usually treated with pharmaceutical drugs, which can cause a number of side effects including drowsiness, agitation, insomnia, sexual dysfunction and headache.

What's more, medications like benzodiazepines can be addictive and may lead to substance abuse.

CBD oil has shown promise as a treatment for both depression and anxiety, leading many who live with these disorders to become interested in this natural approach.

In one Brazilian study, 57 men received either oral CBD or a placebo 90 minutes before they underwent a simulated public speaking test. The researchers found that a 300-mg dose of CBD was the most effective at significantly reducing anxiety during the test.

The placebo, a 150-mg dose of CBD, and a 600-mg dose of CBD had little to no effect on anxiety.

CBD oil has even been used to safely treat insomnia and anxiety in children with post-traumatic stress disorder.

CBD has also shown antidepressant-like effects in several animal studies.

These qualities are linked to CBD's ability to act on the brain's receptors for serotonin, a neurotransmitter that regulates mood and social behavior. Using CBD has been shown to reduce anxiety and depression in both human and animal studies.

3. Can Alleviate Cancer-Related Symptoms

CBD may help reduce symptoms related to cancer and side effects related to cancer treatment, like nausea, vomiting and pain.

One study looked at the effects of CBD and THC in 177 people with cancer-related pain who did not experience relief from pain medication.

Those treated with an extract containing both compounds experienced a significant reduction in pain compared to those who received only THC extract.

CBD may also help reduce chemotherapy-induced nausea and vomiting, which are among the most common chemotherapy-related side effects for those with cancer.

Though there are drugs that help with these distressing symptoms, they are sometimes ineffective, leading some people to seek alternatives.

A study of 16 people undergoing chemotherapy found that a one-to-one combination of CBD and THC administered via mouth spray reduced chemotherapy-related nausea and vomiting better than standard treatment alone.

Some test-tube and animal studies have even shown that CBD may have anticancer properties. For example, one test-tube study found that concentrated CBD induced cell death in human breast cancer cells.

Another study showed that CBD inhibited the spread of aggressive breast cancer cells in mice.

However, these are test-tube and animal studies, so they can only suggest what might work in people. More studies in humans are needed before conclusions can be made. Though CBD has been shown to help reduce symptoms related to cancer and cancer treatment, and may even have cancer-fighting properties, more research is needed to assess its efficacy and safety.

4. May Reduce Acne

Acne is a common skin condition that affects more than 9% of the population.

It is thought to be caused by a number of factors, including genetics, bacteria, underlying inflammation and the overproduction of sebum, an oily secretion made by sebaceous glands in the skin.

Based on recent scientific studies, CBD oil may help treat acne due to its anti-inflammatory properties and ability to reduce sebum production.

One test-tube study found that CBD oil prevented sebaceous gland cells from secreting excessive sebum, exerted anti-inflammatory actions and prevented the activation of "pro-acne" agents like inflammatory cytokines.

Another study had similar findings, concluding that CBD may be an efficient and safe way to treat acne, thanks in part to its remarkable anti-inflammatory qualities.

Though these results are promising, human studies exploring the effects of CBD on acne are needed. CBD may have beneficial effects on acne due to its anti-inflammatory qualities and its ability to control the overproduction of sebum from the sebaceous glands.

5. Might Have Neuroprotective Properties

Researchers believe that CBD's ability to act on the endocannabinoid system and other brain signaling systems may provide benefits for those with neurological disorders.

In fact, one of the most studied uses for CBD is in treating neurological disorders like epilepsy and multiple sclerosis. Though research in this area is still relatively new, several studies have shown promising results.

Sativex, an oral spray consisting of CBD and THC, has been proven to be a safe and effective way to reduce muscle spasticity in people with multiple sclerosis.

One study found that Sativex reduced spasms in 75% of 276 people with multiple sclerosis who were experiencing muscle spasticity that was resistant to medications.

Another study gave 214 people with severe epilepsy 0.9–2.3 grams of CBD oil per pound (2–5 g/kg) of body weight. Their seizures reduced by a median of 36.5%.

One more study found that CBD oil significantly reduced seizure activity in children with Dravet syndrome, a complex childhood epilepsy disorder, compared to a placebo.

However, it's important to note that some people in both these studies experienced adverse reactions associated with CBD treatment, such as convulsions, fever and fatigue.

CBD has also been researched for its potential effectiveness in treating several other neurological diseases.

For example, several studies have shown that treatment with CBD improved quality of life and sleep quality for people with Parkinson's disease (29Trusted Source, 30Trusted Source).

Additionally, animal and test-tube studies have shown that CBD may decrease inflammation and help prevent the neurodegeneration associated with Alzheimer's disease.

In one long-term study, researchers gave CBD to mice genetically predisposed to Alzheimer's disease, finding that it helped prevent cognitive decline. Though research is limited at this time, CBD has been shown to ease symptoms related to epilepsy and Parkinson's disease. CBD was also shown to reduce the progression of Alzheimer's disease in test-tube and animal studies.

6. Could Benefit Heart Health

Recent research has linked CBD with several benefits for the heart and circulatory system, including the ability to lower high blood pressure.

High blood pressure is linked to higher risks of a number of health conditions, including stroke, heart attack and metabolic syndrome.

Studies indicate that CBD may be able to help with high blood pressure.

One recent study treated nine healthy men with one dose of 600 mg of CBD oil and found it reduced resting blood pressure, compared to a placebo.

The same study also gave the men stress tests that normally increase blood pressure. Interestingly, the single dose of CBD led the men to experience a smaller blood pressure increase than normal in response to these test.

Researchers have suggested that the stress- and anxiety-reducing properties of CBD are responsible for its ability to help lower blood pressure.

Additionally, several animal studies have demonstrated that CBD may help reduce the inflammation and cell death associated with heart disease due to its powerful antioxidant and stress-reducing properties.

For example, one study found that treatment with CBD reduced oxidative stress and prevented heart damage in diabetic mice with heart disease. Though more human studies are needed, CBD may benefit heart health in several ways, including by reducing blood pressure and preventing heart damage.

7. Several Other Potential Benefits

CBD has been studied for its role in treating a number of health issues other than those outlined above.

Though more studies are needed, CBD is thought to provide the following health benefits:

- Antipsychotic effects: Studies suggest that CBD may help people with schizophrenia and other mental disorders by reducing psychotic symptoms.

- Substance abuse treatment: CBD has been shown to modify circuits in the brain related to drug addiction. In rats, CBD has been shown to reduce morphine dependence and heroin-seeking behavior.

• Anti-tumor effects: In test-tube and animal studies, CBD has demonstrated anti-tumor effects. In animals, it has been shown to prevent the spread of breast, prostate, brain, colon and lung cancer.

• Diabetes prevention: In diabetic mice, treatment with CBD reduced the incidence of diabetes by 56% and significantly reduced inflammation. Some studies suggest that CBD may help with diabetes, substance abuse, mental disorders and certain types of cancers. However, more research in humans is needed.

Is CBD marijuana?

CBD oil may have a number of health benefits. Until recently, the best-known compound in cannabis was delta-9 tetrahydrocannabinol (THC). This is the most active constituent of marijuana.

Marijuana contains both THC and CBD, and these compounds have different effects.

THC creates a mind-altering "high" when a person smokes it or uses it in cooking. This is because THC breaks down when we apply heat and introduce it into the body.

CBD is different. Unlike THC, it is not psychoactive. This means that CBD does not change a person's state of mind when they use it.

However, CBD does appear to produce significant changes in the body, and some research suggests that it has medical benefits.

Where does CBD come from?

CBD comes from the cannabis plant. People refer to cannabis plants as either hemp or marijuana, depending on their level of THC. Hemp plants that are legal under the Farm Bill must contain less than 0.3% THC.

Over the years, marijuana farmers have selectively bred their plants to contain high levels of THC and other compounds that interested them, often because the compounds produced a smell or had another effect on the plant's flowers.

However, hemp farmers have rarely modified the plant. These hemp plants are used to create CBD oil.

How CBD works

All cannabinoids, including CBD, produce effects in the body by attaching to certain receptors.

The human body produces certain cannabinoids on its own. It also has two receptors for cannabinoids, called the CB1 receptors and CB2 receptors.

CB1 receptors are present throughout the body, but many are in the brain.

The CB1 receptors in the brain deal with coordination and movement, pain, emotions, and mood, thinking, appetite, and memories, and other functions. THC attaches to these receptors.

CB2 receptors are more common in the immune system. They affect inflammation and pain.

Researchers once believed that CBD attached to these CB2 receptors, but it now appears that CBD does not attach directly to either receptor.

Instead, it seems to direct the body to use more of its own cannabinoids.

Benefits

CBD may benefit a person's health in a variety of ways.

Natural pain relief and anti-inflammatory properties

People tend to use prescription or over-the-counter drugs to relieve stiffness and pain, including chronic pain.

Some people believe that CBD offers a more natural alternative.

Authors of a study published in the Journal of Experimental Medicine found that CBD significantly reduced chronic inflammation and pain in some mice and rats.

The researchers suggested that the non-psychoactive compounds in marijuana, such as CBD, could provide a new treatment for chronic pain.

Quitting smoking and drug withdrawals

Some promising evidence suggests that CBD use may help people to quit smoking.

A pilot studyTrusted Source published in Addictive Behaviors found that smokers who used inhalers containing CBD smoked fewer cigarettes than usual and had no further cravings for nicotine.

A similar review,Trusted Source published in Neurotherapeutics found that CBD may be a promising treatment for people with opioid addiction disorders.

The researchers noted that CBD reduced some symptoms associated with substance use disorders. These included anxiety, mood-related symptoms, pain, and insomnia.

More research is necessary, but these findings suggest that CBD may help to prevent or reduce withdrawal symptoms.

Epilepsy

After researching the safety and effectiveness of CBD oil for treating epilepsy, the FDA approved the use of CBD (Epidiolex) as a therapyTrusted Source for two rare conditions characterized by epileptic seizures in 2018.

In the U.S., a doctor can prescribe Epidiolex to treat:

- Lennox-Gastaut syndrome (LGS), a condition that appears between the ages of 3 and 5 years and involves different kinds of seizures

- Dravet syndrome (DS), a rare genetic condition that appears in the first year of life and involves frequent, fever-related seizures

The types of seizures that characterize LGS or DS are difficult to control with other types of medication.

The FDA specified that doctors could not prescribe Epidiolex for children younger than 2 yearsTrusted

Source. A physician or pharmacist will determine the right dosage based on body weight.

Other neurological symptoms and disorders

Researchers are studying the effects of CBD on various neuropsychiatric disorders.

Findings suggested that CBD may also treat many complications linked to epilepsy, such as neurodegeneration, neuronal injury, and psychiatric diseases.

Another study,Trusted Source published in Current Pharmaceutical Design, found that CBD may produce effects similar to those of certain antipsychotic drugs, and that the compound may provide a safe and effective treatment for people with schizophrenia. However, further research is necessary.

Risks

There is still a lack of available long-term safety data.

Also, to date, researchers have not performed studies involving children.

Side effects of other uses of CBD

There is often a lack of evidence regarding the safety of new or alternative treatment options. Usually, researchers have not performed the full array of tests.

Anyone who is considering using CBD should talk to a qualified healthcare practitioner beforehand.

The FDA have only approved CBD for the treatment of two rare and severe forms of epilepsy.

When drugs do not have FDA approval, it can be difficultTrusted Source to know whether a product contains a safe or effective level of CBD.

Unapproved products may not have the properties or contents stated on the packaging.

It is important to note that researchers have linked marijuana use during pregnancy to impairmentsTrusted Source in the fetal development of neurons. Regular use among teens is associated with issues concerning memory, behavior, and intelligence.

How to use
CBD is just one of may compounds in marijuana, and it is not psychoactive. Smoking cannabis is not the same as using CBD oil.

Using CBD oil is not the same as using or smoking whole cannabis.

A person can use CBD oil in different ways to relieve various symptoms. If a doctor prescribes it to treat LGS or DS, it is important to follow their instructions.

CBD-based products come in many forms. Some can be mixed into different foods or drinks or taken with a pipette or dropper.

Others are available in capsules or as a thick paste to be massaged into the skin. Some products are available as sprays to be administered under the tongue.

Recommended dosages vary between individuals, and depend on factors such as body weight, the concentration of the product, and the health issue.

Some people consider taking CBD oil to help treat:

• chronic pain

• epilepsy

• Parkinson's disease

• Huntington's disease

• sleep disorders

- glaucoma

Due to the lack of FDA regulation for most CBD products, seek advice from a medical professional before determining the best dosage.

As regulation in the U.S. increases, more specific dosages and prescriptions will start to emerge.

After discussing dosages and risks with a doctor, and researching regional local laws, it is important to compare different brands of CBD oil.

The Difference Between CBD and THC

Cannabidiol (CBD) and tetrahydrocannabinol (THC) are the two most prominent cannabinoids found in Cannabis, the plant genus that includes both hemp and marijuana. While there are over 100 different cannabinoids so far identified in cannabis by scientists, CBD and THC are by far the most extensively studied and best understood.

One of the key differences between CBD and THC is whether the cannabinoid will cause a euphoric effect, or "high," when consumed. THC does, and CBD does not have the "high" effect when consumed.

CBD and THC both interact with the body through the endocannabinoid system, a vital signaling system responsible for regulating a wide array of functions.

Both plant-derived cannabinoids like CBD and THC and the body's own endocannabinoids interact with this regulatory network through its cannabinoid receptors, found all throughout the body. A well operating endocannabinoid promotes health and well-being.

How CBD Oil Makes You Feel

First and foremost, CBD will not cause you to experience a euphoric effect, or "high." It is completely non-psychoactive. This means that unlike THC, supplementing with CBD oil will not adversely affect you or your wellbeing.

Our CBD oil comes from hemp, which contains no more than 0.3% THC per dry weight, far too low to get a user "high."

CBD Oil Serving Sizes & Safety

Our rigorous quality control processes ensure the safety and reliability of our CBD oil products. Our CBD oil comes from non-GMO hemp grown without the use of pesticides or chemical fertilizers, and is tested three separate times throughout manufacturing to verify its quality and safety. For more information see our guide to CBD oil serving sizes.

Harvesting and transport
After seasonal harvests of specific cultivars, these high-CBD hemp crops are put through a specialized solvent-free extraction process to yield a hemp oil that is naturally high in cannabidiol. This high CBD oil is different from hemp oil that is used in cooking. This pure hemp extract is then tested for safety, quality, and cannabinoid content before being exported to our processing facilities in the United States. Importing any cannabis or hemp product into the United States is a complicated and serious task, so we leave nothing to chance before our high-CBD hemp oil makes its journey across the Atlantic Ocean.

After clearing U.S. Customs inspection, we test the hemp oil again when it reaches our facilities. After a 10,000+ mile transcontinental trip, we follow proper safety protocol to double check for degradation, damage, or contamination in our oil.

Finally, the imported bulk CBD hemp oil is combined with other ingredients by our formulators to create our extensive lineup of internationally recognized brands, like Dixie Botanicals®, CanChew®, and Real Scientific Hemp Oil™.

The finished products are then tested for a final time to once again ensure the safety, quality, and cannabinoid content of our products. This is our standard Triple Lab Testing® process that all our CBD oil products complete.

In the natural product and dietary supplement industries, these rigorous testing practices are not required by regulations — but nothing is more important to us than the quality of the products we provide our customers.

What is Epidiolex?

Epidiolex (cannabidiol) is a prescription medicine used to treat seizures in people with Lennox-Gastaut syndrome or Dravet syndrome. Epidiolex is for use in adults and children who are at least 2 years old.

Epidiolex is controlled in Schedule V of the Controlled Substances Act. Keep this medicine in a safe place to prevent misuse and abuse.

Important Information

You should not use Epidiolex if you are allergic to cannabidiol or sesame seed oil. Cannabidiol can harm your liver. Your liver function may need to be checked before and during treatment.

Call your doctor at once if you have symptoms such as: nausea, vomiting, loss of appetite, right-sided upper stomach pain, tiredness, itching, dark urine, or yellowing of the skin or eyes. Avoid driving or hazardous activity until you know how Epidiolex will affect you.

Some people have thoughts about suicide while taking Epidiolex. Stay alert to changes in your mood or symptoms. Report any new or worsening symptoms to your doctor.

Before taking this medicine
Epidiolex is not approved for use by anyone younger than 2 years old. To make sure Epidiolex is safe for you, tell your doctor if you have ever had:

• liver disease;

• drug or alcohol addiction;

• depression, a mood disorder; or

• suicidal thoughts or actions.

Some people have thoughts about suicide while taking Epidiolex. Your doctor will need to check your progress at regular visits. Your family or other caregivers should also be alert to changes in your mood or symptoms.

It is not known whether cannabidiol will harm an unborn baby. Tell your doctor if you are pregnant or plan to become pregnant.

If you are pregnant, your name may be listed on a pregnancy registry to track the effects of cannabidiol on the baby.

It may not be safe to breast-feed while using Epidiolex. Ask your doctor about any risk.

How should I take Epidiolex?

Take Epidiolex exactly as prescribed by your doctor. Follow all directions on your prescription label and read all medication guides or instruction sheets. Your doctor may occasionally change your dose. Use the medicine exactly as directed.

Epidiolex is usually taken 2 times per day. Take the medicine at the same times each day.

You may take Epidiolex with or without food, but take it the same way each time.

Measure this medicine carefully. Use the dosing syringe provided, or use a medicine dose-measuring device (not a kitchen spoon). Make sure the dosing syringe is completely dry before measuring your dose.

Cannabidiol can harm your liver. Your liver function may need to be checked before and during treatment. You may need to stop taking Epidiolex based on the results.

Store at room temperature, away from moisture and heat. Do not refrigerate or freeze. Keep the bottle tightly closed and in an upright position when not in use.

Throw away any unused liquid 12 weeks after you first opened the bottle.

Epidiolex can affect a drug-screening test and you may test positive for cannabis (marijuana). Tell the laboratory staff that you use cannabidiol.

Do not stop using Epidiolex suddenly, even if you feel fine. Stopping suddenly may cause increased seizures. Follow your doctor's instructions about tapering your dose.

Epidiolex Dosing Information

Usual Adult Dose of Epidiolex for Lennox-Gastaut Syndrome:

Initial dose: 2.5 mg/kg orally twice a day

-After 1 week, may increase dose to 5 mg/kg orally twice a day; for patients tolerating therapy and requiring further reduction in seizures, dose may be increased in increments of 2.5 mg/kg twice a day, as tolerated but no more frequently than every other day to 20 mg/kg/day

Maintenance dose: 10 to 20 mg/kg/day

Maximum dose: 20 mg/kg/day

Comments:

-A dose of 20 mg/kg /day has demonstrated a greater reduction in seizure rates, but with an increase in adverse reactions.

-Dose should be measured with a calibrated measuring device to ensure accuracy in dosing.

Use: For the treatment of seizures associated with Lennox-Gastaut syndrome or Dravet syndrome in patients 2 years of age and older.

Usual Adult Dose of Epidiolex for Dravet Syndrome:

Initial dose: 2.5 mg/kg orally twice a day

-After 1 week, may increase dose to 5 mg/kg orally twice a day; for patients tolerating therapy and requiring further reduction in seizures, dose may be increased in increments of 2.5 mg/kg twice a day, as tolerated but no more frequently than every other day to 20 mg/kg/day

Maintenance dose: 10 to 20 mg/kg/day

Maximum dose: 20 mg/kg/day

Comments:

-A dose of 20 mg/kg /day has demonstrated a greater reduction in seizure rates, but with an increase in adverse reactions.

-Dose should be measured with a calibrated measuring device to ensure accuracy in dosing.

Use: For the treatment of seizures associated with Lennox-Gastaut syndrome or Dravet syndrome in patients 2 years of age and older.

Usual Pediatric Dose for Lennox-Gastaut Syndrome:

2 years or older:

Initial dose: 2.5 mg/kg orally twice a day

-After 1 week, may increase dose to 5 mg/kg orally twice a day; for patients tolerating therapy and requiring further reduction in seizures, dose may be increased in increments of 2.5 mg/kg twice a day, as tolerated but no more frequently than every other day to 20 mg/kg/day

Maintenance dose: 10 to 20 mg/kg/day

Maximum dose: 20 mg/kg/day

Comments:

-A dose of 20 mg/kg /day has demonstrated a greater reduction in seizure rates, but with an increase in adverse reactions.

-Dose should be measured with a calibrated measuring device to ensure accuracy in dosing.

Use: For the treatment of seizures associated with Lennox-Gastaut syndrome or Dravet syndrome in patients 2 years of age and older.

Usual Pediatric Dose for Dravet Syndrome:

2 years or older:

Initial dose: 2.5 mg/kg orally twice a day

-After 1 week, may increase dose to 5 mg/kg orally twice a day; for patients tolerating therapy and requiring further reduction in seizures, dose may be increased in increments of 2.5 mg/kg twice a day, as tolerated but no more frequently than every other day to 20 mg/kg/day

Maintenance dose: 10 to 20 mg/kg/day

Maximum dose: 20 mg/kg/day

Comments:

-A dose of 20 mg/kg /day has demonstrated a greater reduction in seizure rates, but with an increase in adverse reactions.

-Dose should be measured with a calibrated measuring device to ensure accuracy in dosing.

Use: For the treatment of seizures associated with Lennox-Gastaut syndrome or Dravet syndrome in patients 2 years of age and older.

What happens if I miss a dose?
Take the medicine as soon as you can, but skip the missed dose if it is almost time for your next dose. Do not take two doses at one time.

What happens if I overdose?
Seek emergency medical attention or call the Poison Help line at 1-800-222-1222.

What should I avoid while taking Epidiolex?
Drinking alcohol with Epidiolex can increase drowsiness.

Avoid driving or hazardous activity until you know how this medicine will affect you. Dizziness or drowsiness can cause falls, accidents, or severe injuries.

What other drugs will affect Epidiolex?

Using Epidiolex with other drugs that make you drowsy can worsen this effect. Ask your doctor before using opioid medication, a sleeping pill, a muscle relaxer, or medicine for anxiety or seizures.

Sometimes it is not safe to use certain medications at the same time. Some drugs can affect your blood levels of other drugs you take, which may increase side effects or make the medications less effective.

Tell your doctor about all your other medicines, especially:

• other seizure medications; or

• cannabis-based products.

This list is not complete. Many other drugs can interact with cannabidiol, including prescription and over-the-counter medicines, vitamins, and herbal products. Not all possible interactions are listed here. Tell your doctor about all your current medicines and any medicine you start or stop using.

Remember, keep this and all other medicines out of the reach of children, never share your medicines with others, and use Epidiolex only for the indication prescribed.

Always consult your healthcare provider to ensure the information displayed on this page applies to your personal circumstances.

What's the difference between Epidiolex and other CBD products?

Families whose children suffer seizures from epilepsy have asked legislators in several states to "legalize" cannabidiol (CBD), "medicinal" marijuana, and "whole-plant extracts" so they can use them to reduce their children's seizures. The marijuana industry has been happy to accommodate, helping parents lobby legislators and, when successful, producing CBD products.

But none of these products is approved by FDA as safe or effective. All make unsubstantiated medical claims. Few contain what their labels claim. Some contain contaminants. Recently, the Centers for Disease Control and Prevention reported that 52 people in Utah were poisoned by an unregulated CBD product, which contained a synthetic cannabinoid. The agency warned regulations are needed to address "this emerging public health threat."

This week, FDA approved Epidiolex to treat two forms of epilepsy in patients ages 2 and older. Epidiolex is an extract of marijuana called cannabidiol (CBD) that is purified and delivers a reliable, consistent dose. Clinical trials proved it reduces epileptic seizures. Now families have a choice. They no longer need to risk giving their children unregulated products that may harm their already fragile health.

Epidiolex

• FDA approved

• Proven to be safe

• Proven to reduce seizures

• A purified extract of marijuana that is 99% CBD, less than 1% THC, marijuana's psychoactive ingredient

• Doctors prescribe.

• Patients buy at pharmacies.

• Likely to be insured.

• Likely moved to a lower Schedule CBD Products States Have Legalized

• Not FDA approved

- Not proven to be safe

- Not proven to reduce seizures

- Unpurified extracts containing up to 20% CBD, THC, other components. Some are contaminated.

- Doctors recommend.

- Patients buy at dispensaries.

- Not insured.

- Likely to remain in Schedule 1

Many media outlets are reporting that FDA's approval of Epidiolex means CBD will be placed in a lower schedule of the federal Controlled Substances Act. But FDA Commissioner Scott Gottlieb clarifies, "This is the approval of one specific CBD medication for a specific use . . . based on well-controlled clinical trials evaluating the use of this compound in the treatment of a specific condition." Just as Marinol, Cesamet, and Syndros,

FDA-approved forms of THC, are in lower schedules but THC remains in Schedule I, Epidiolex is likely to be placed in a lower Schedule while CBD likely will remain in Schedule I.

Commissioner Gottlieb says FDA continues to support rigorous scientific research into potential medical treatments using marijuana or its components but is concerned about the proliferation and illegal marketing of unapproved CBD-containing products making unproven medical claims. FDA will continue to act to end such behavior, he says.

Action is certainly needed. Searching for CBD Oil on Amazon brings up 929 results. All unregulated.

FDA approves first drug comprised of an active ingredient derived from marijuana to treat rare, severe forms of epilepsy

The U.S. Food and Drug Administration today approved Epidiolex (cannabidiol) [CBD] oral solution for the treatment of seizures associated with two rare and severe forms of epilepsy, Lennox-Gastaut syndrome and Dravet syndrome, in patients two years of age and older. This is the first FDA-approved drug that contains a purified drug substance derived from marijuana. It is also the first FDA approval of a drug for the treatment of patients with Dravet syndrome.

CBD is a chemical component of the Cannabis sativa plant, more commonly known as marijuana. However, CBD does not cause intoxication or euphoria (the "high") that comes from tetrahydrocannabinol (THC). It is THC (and not CBD) that is the primary psychoactive component of marijuana.

"This approval serves as a reminder that advancing sound development programs that properly evaluate active ingredients contained in marijuana can lead to important medical therapies. And, the FDA is committed to this kind of careful scientific research and drug development," said FDA Commissioner Scott Gottlieb, M.D. "Controlled clinical trials testing the safety and efficacy of a drug, along with careful review through the FDA's drug approval process, is the most appropriate way to bring marijuana-derived treatments to patients. Because of the adequate and well-controlled clinical studies that supported this approval, prescribers can have confidence in the drug's uniform strength and consistent delivery that support appropriate dosing needed for treating patients with these complex and serious epilepsy syndromes. We'll continue to support rigorous scientific research on the potential medical uses of marijuana-derived products and work with product developers who are interested in bringing patients safe and effective, high quality products. But, at the same time, we are prepared to take action when we see the illegal marketing of CBD-containing products with serious, unproven medical claims. Marketing unapproved products, with uncertain dosages and formulations can keep patients from accessing appropriate, recognized therapies to treat serious and even fatal diseases."

Dravet syndrome is a rare genetic condition that appears during the first year of life with frequent fever-related seizures (febrile seizures). Later, other types of seizures typically arise, including myoclonic seizures (involuntary muscle spasms). Additionally, status epilepticus, a potentially life-threatening state of continuous seizure activity requiring emergency medical care, may occur. Children with Dravet syndrome typically experience poor development of language and motor skills, hyperactivity and difficulty relating to others.

Lennox-Gastaut syndrome begins in childhood. It is characterized by multiple types of seizures. People with Lennox-Gastaut syndrome begin having frequent seizures in early childhood, usually between ages 3 and 5. More than three-quarters of affected individuals have tonic seizures, which cause the muscles to contract uncontrollably. Almost all children with Lennox-Gastaut syndrome develop learning problems and intellectual disability. Many also have delayed development of motor skills such as sitting and crawling. Most people with Lennox-Gastaut syndrome require help with usual activities of daily living.

"The difficult-to-control seizures that patients with Dravet syndrome and Lennox-Gastaut syndrome experience have a profound impact on these patients' quality of life," said Billy Dunn, M.D., director of the Division of Neurology Products in the FDA's Center for Drug Evaluation and Research. "In addition to another important treatment option for Lennox-Gastaut patients, this first-ever approval of a drug specifically for Dravet patients will provide a significant and needed improvement in the therapeutic approach to caring for people with this condition."

Epidiolex's effectiveness was studied in three randomized, double-blind, placebo-controlled clinical trials involving 516 patients with either Lennox-Gastaut syndrome or Dravet syndrome. Epidiolex, taken along with other medications, was shown to be effective in reducing the frequency of seizures when compared with placebo.

The most common side effects that occurred in Epidiolex-treated patients in the clinical trials were: sleepiness, sedation and lethargy; elevated liver enzymes; decreased appetite; diarrhea; rash; fatigue, malaise and weakness; insomnia, sleep disorder and poor quality sleep; and infections.

Epidiolex must be dispensed with a patient Medication Guide that describes important information about the drug's uses and risks. As is true for all drugs that treat epilepsy, the most serious risks include thoughts about suicide, attempts to commit suicide, feelings of agitation, new or worsening depression, aggression and panic attacks. Epidiolex also caused liver injury, generally mild, but raising the possibility of rare, but more severe injury. More severe liver injury can cause nausea, vomiting, abdominal pain, fatigue, anorexia, jaundice and/or dark urine.

Under the Controlled Substances Act (CSA), CBD is currently a Schedule I substance because it is a chemical component of the cannabis plant. In support of this application, the company conducted nonclinical and clinical studies to assess the abuse potential of CBD.

The FDA prepares and transmits, through the U.S. Department of Health and Human Services, a medical and scientific analysis of substances subject to scheduling, like CBD, and provides recommendations to the Drug Enforcement Administration (DEA) regarding controls under the CSA. DEA is required to make a scheduling determination.

The FDA granted Priority Review designation for this application. Fast-Trackdesignation was granted for Dravet syndrome. Orphan Drug designation was granted for both the Dravet syndrome and Lennox-Gastaut syndrome indications.

The FDA granted approval of Epidiolex to GW Research Ltd.

The FDA, an agency within the U.S. Department of Health and Human Services, protects the public health by assuring the safety, effectiveness, and security of human and veterinary drugs, vaccines and other biological products for human use, and medical devices. The agency also is responsible for the safety and security of our nation's food supply, cosmetics, dietary supplements, products that give off electronic radiation, and for regulating tobacco products.

How Does the FDA Approval Process Work?

Hundreds of people like you or your loved one participated in the clinical trials that helped the FDA evaluate the safety, effectiveness, and dosing of EPIDIOLEX. These studies were all part of the FDA's rigorous process to evaluate a potential medicine. This process includes regular inspections and consultations with the manufacturer to validate the clinical study program and quality control during production.

Greenwich Biosciences worked with the FDA for years to bring the first prescription cannabidiol (CBD) medicine to US patients in 2018.

Take a closer look at the FDA approval process.

First Steps

- Led by the treatment manufacturer, discovery and development begins

- New compounds are identified

- Preliminary preclinical research is initiated

STEP 1

Early Testing

- The treatment manufacturer begins lab studies and animal testing

- Basic safety is evaluated

- Human studies begin to be planned

STEP 2

Human Testing

- Investigational New Drug applications are submitted to the FDA based on preclinical study results

- The treatment manufacturer oversees human trials that test for safety, efficacy, and dosing in 100s to 1000s of patients

- Inspections are conducted by the FDA to confirm a company's clinical and manufacturing processes meet FDA standards

STEP 3

Data Review

- The data from the trials are summarized and submitted as a New Drug Application (NDA) to the FDA

- The FDA thoroughly examines all of the submitted data in the NDA to decide whether a treatment should be approved

STEP 4

Ongoing Monitoring

• Once approved and available, the FDA continues to monitor the manufacturing and adverse events of a medication, as well as any communication to the public

• Additional studies may be conducted to provide more information

CHAPTER TWO

Dog Seizures:

Seizures in dogs can be scary when they first happen, but as with many other medical conditions, if they are properly managed they needn't affect your dear pooch's quality of life—or yours.

If your pet has an unexplained seizure, it is very important that you take them to the vet as soon as possible, as symptoms can worsen if left untreated.

What Causes Seizures in Dogs

There are a number of different types of seizures that dogs can have, and these can be caused by many different things. Identifying the kind of seizure is important for successful treatment or management.

Environmental causes of canine seizures include eating something poisonous (such as caffeine, chocolate, toxic plants, cleaning products and more) or head injuries. Environmental causes are the easiest to avoid, and if you have a pet dog, you should always try to minimize risks in your home.

Some dogs are more genetically prone to seizures than others. Breeds more prone to developing genetic seizure disorders include Belgian Tervurens, Irish wolfhounds, German shepherds, Labrador retrievers, Bernese mountain dogs and English springer spaniels. Before you get a certain breed of dog, it is worth asking your vet whether they are more prone to seizures.

Seizures in Small Dogs

Puppies and small dogs can be more prone to seizures. Some will grow out of them, and others will keep having them for the rest of their lives. Sometimes, sadly, these seizures are caused by disease, but the most common cause of seizures in puppies and young dogs is epilepsy. Most dogs begin to have epileptic seizures between the ages of six months and six years.

Seizures in Older Dogs

If an older dog has never shown signs of epilepsy, it is unlikely that it will present in a senior dog; the seizures are more likely to be caused by a disease.

There are a number of illnesses that can cause seizures in your pet. These include kidney or liver disease, brain cancer, anemia, low or high blood pressure, encephalitis, and others, If your pet's seizures are caused by illness, it is important that your veterinarian treats the underlying cause of the seizures as well, not just the symptoms.

Another factor to consider when an older dog has seizures is that they can be frailer, and more likely to get hurt or disoriented. Take extra care to keep your senior pet safe and comfortable if it starts having seizures.

Can They Have Epileptic Seizures

If your dog has recurrent seizures, this is known as epilepsy. When canine epilepsy has a known cause (such as disease), it is called secondary epilepsy. However, some pets will have recurring epileptic seizures that are unexplained, and this is known as idiopathic epilepsy or primary epilepsy.

Although idiopathic epilepsy in dogs is not treatable, the symptoms can be managed through a combination of anti-seizure medication and lifestyle changes, and epileptic dogs can still enjoy a good quality of life.

A Scary Situation for Pet Owners

Symptoms of Seizures in Dogs

Whether it is your pet's first seizure or its 50th, it can be very upsetting. Learning to spot the symptoms can help you to prepare yourself and your pet.

What To Watch Out For—Dog Seizure Symptoms

The most common type of seizure is generalized, tonic-clonic or grand mal seizures. Many dogs experience generalized seizures in three stages, though this is not always the case.

• The pre-ictal or aura phase comes first, and it is thought that this is when your dog senses that something is about to happen. You may notice your pet acting strangely: nervousness, confusion, distraction, and unsteadiness are all signs that a seizure is coming. This stage may last anywhere from mere seconds to a few hours.

• The next stage in a grand mal seizure is the ictal stage, and this is the easiest to spot. Your dog may collapse and lose consciousness, and begin making involuntary jerking movements that can look like running on the spot. They may drool or foam at the mouth, and can sometimes chomp or chew their tongues. Some dogs will evacuate their bowels during a seizure.

If a dog's seizure activity last more than five minutes, or if it has multiple seizures in a short time without fully regaining consciousness, this is known as status epilepticus. Status epilepticus is a life-threatening condition and you should contact your veterinarian immediately.

• The final or post-ictal period is the period immediately following the seizure, when your pet may experience confusion, restlessness, distress, and in some cases temporary blindness. The amount of time this phase lasts can vary and is not directly linked to the severity of the tonic-clonic seizures.

Types of Seizures in Dogs

In addition, the generalized tonic-clonic seizures described above, there are other kinds of seizures to watch out for. Mild seizures are similar to generalized seizures but without the loss of consciousness or such pronounced spasms.

Petit mal seizures in dogs are manifested by brief absences and can be difficult to spot. Look out for short periods of unconsciousness, upturned eyes, or blank stares.

Cluster Seizures in Dogs

Cluster seizures is a term to describe multiple seizures that happen within a 24-hour period. Although the individual seizures may be brief, cluster seizures are considered life-threatening and you should contact your vet immediately if your pet has them.

Focal Seizures in Dogs

Focal seizures or partial seizures occur when there is irregular activity in just one area of the brain. They can remain partial or spread to the rest of the brain and develop into generalized seizures. Again, focal seizures could be more difficult to spot, but symptoms include twitching or jerking on one side of the body, along with restlessness and distractedness.

Complex partial seizures are where the dog's consciousness in more impaired, but not fully lost.

Idiopathic Epilepsy

These seizures occur due to some unknown cause. They usually develop in dogs between the age of 6 months to 6 years.

Idiopathic epilepsy does not affect the brain and most commonly occurs in beagles, Australian shepherds, German shepherds, collies, Labrador retrievers, and Belgian Tervurens.

Psychomotor Seizure

A psychomotor seizure is associated with a specific strange behavior that lasts for a few minutes. Differentiating between an odd expression and a psychomotor seizure is difficult.

Usually, a dog having psychomotor seizure starts chasing its tail or any imaginary object and always act the same every time it undergoes a seizure.

Can Dog Seizures Be Cured, Stopped, or Prevented?

The short answer to this question is, it depends.

• Idiopathic epilepsy cannot be treated, but the symptoms can be managed and the seizures can be controlled. Some pets will stop having seizures as they mature.

• Secondary epilepsy in dogs can sometimes be treated by addressing the underlying cause, though this is not always possible.

• With careful management and the right medication (see below), the frequency and severity of seizures can be reduced significantly.

How to Stop a Dog Seizure
There is some debate about whether you should try to stop your pet's seizure once it has already started,

especially if it has frequent seizures that are predictable and manageable.

Diazepam (the generic name for Valium) can be given to stop a seizure in progress or to stop cluster seizures from happening once the first one has finished. Diazepam is usually administered via an intravenous drip or rectally. However, this medication loses its efficiency when used daily, so should not be used as the main method or treating seizures in dogs. Always consult with your vet before beginning a new medication.

Some people swear by homeopathic methods to stop seizures in dogs. These include placing an icepack on the small of its back, or holding the dog and using a particular command (for example, "Stay with me!") to help the dog regain control. There are a number of videos illustrating this technique on Youtube.

Tips on how to Handle Dog Seizures

1. Don't move a dog if it is having a seizure, as you could hurt it or yourself. Only move a dog while it is having a seizure if it is in immediate danger.

2. Clear debris away from your dog to keep it safe and comfortable.

3. Time your dog's seizures. If they last more than five minutes, contact your vet.

4. Comfort your dog by stroking it or speaking to it, but be sure to keep your hands clear of its mouth as it may bite down hard when its muscles spasm.

5. Dogs may urinate or defecate uncontrollably during a seizure, so you may want to put down newspaper or plastic sheeting if you can do so without disturbing your dog.

6. Many dogs will be hungry after a seizure, so make sure that there are food and water available. If the seizures are caused by low blood sugar, feeding

your dog something sugary like honey can help to bring their glucose levels up quickly.

7. Monitor your dog's health afterwards. It may be distressed or confused, so make sure you are there to comfort it. Keep a note of any other symptoms, and contact your vet if you are concerned.

Dog Seizure Medication

The most common treatments for treating seizures in dogs are potassium bromide, phenobarbital and, more recently, CBD.

• Potassium bromide is a reliable drug that is easy to use. It is usually given once a day with a meal. Some dogs may experience side-effects from potassium bromide, including an upset stomach, stumbling and drowsiness. Dogs that are taking potassium bromide should avoid excess salt in their diet as it can interfere with absorption of the drug. They will also need to be given regular blood tests to check the potassium bromide in their blood levels.

- Phenobarbital is the most common anti-epileptic drug for dogs. It can be used both to prevent seizures and to stop seizures in progress. It is usually given twice a day. Most dogs do not experience side-effects on phenobarbital, but those that do may be more drowsy or unsteady, or experience increased appetite, which can lead to obesity.

- CBD Oil has increased in popularity recently after initial positive testing in humans. While the exact mechanism for reduction is still debated, veterinarians are increasingly recommending it as a potential alternative to reduce the frequency of occurrences.

You should always consult with your veterinarian if you think your dog's medication should be changed. Never stop giving medication suddenly—instead, reduce the dose gradually.

Natural Remedies for Dog Seizures

What Are They? Can they work?

Some dog owners swear by natural treatments for their epileptic dogs, though the scientific backing behind them is sometimes lacking. These natural remedies can include belladonna, aconite, cocculus, silica, Hyoscyamus, kali brom, bufo and cicuta virosa. Always check with your vet before starting new anticonvulsant medication.

Dog Seizure Treatment Home Remedy

If you don't want to try a homeopathic treatment, there are still a number of methods you can try to improve your dog's overall health, which could help to manage its seizures.

• Improve your dog's diet: try to avoid "human food" or overly processed dog food, and opt instead for more natural ingredients. Cooked chicken and rice are good for fussy eaters, or ask your vet to recommend healthier brands of dog food. Some owners even opt for raw meat and bones or a ketogenic diet that is low in carbohydrates.

• Boost your dog's immune system with vitamins and supplements—but check with your veterinarian beforehand. Vitamins C, E and B6, as well as magnesium, have all been linked to stronger immune systems.

• Consider alternative therapies: some owners have sworn by remedies such as acupuncture, homeopathy, magnets and herbal medicines to help treat their pet's seizures.

• Increase the amount of exercise and fresh air that your dog gets. It can boost their mood and fitness—and it might help yours too!

How to Gain Seizure Control

While seizures in dogs can be scary for pet and owner alike, it is important to remember that epileptic dogs can still enjoy a long and happy life.

Once your vet has established the reason behind your dog's seizures, there are many ways to manage them. You will find yourself getting into a routine that will help you maintain seizure control each time your pet is afflicted. Dogs can sense stress, and if you are able to remain calm, you will be more able to help them through it.

The Basics of Dog Seizures

Before talking about treatment options, it's important to first discuss what causes seizures in dogs and how it affects them. Abnormal, uncontrolled bursts of electrical activity in a dog's brain cause seizures that affect how your pup looks and behaves. Seizures may be isolated or recurring (which is typically indicative of a medical issue or disorder, such as canine epilepsy). Seizures can last up to several minutes and can be scary for everyone. There are several causes of seizures including:

- Kidney disease

- Liver disease

- Abnormal blood sugar levels

- Head injury

- Ingesting poison

- Brain cancer

- Electrolyte problems

- Anemia

- Epilepsy

Common symptoms include collapsing, stiffening, muscle twitching, drooling, and foaming at the mouth. If your dog experiences a seizure, it's important to stay calm and gently move him away from anything that may result in injury.

If the seizure lasts more than a couple of minutes, your dog may be at risk of overheating. In this case, you can put cold water on their paws to help cool them down. Once the seizure has passed, you'll need to bring your pup to the vet. Your vet will likely perform a thorough examination and run some lab work to determine possible causes and best options of treatment moving forward.

An Effective Treatment Method

Medications are commonly prescribed to help control future seizures, especially in circumstances where dogs experience frequent seizures or have a disorder that needs to be managed such as epilepsy. However, CBD oil for dog seizures can be a highly effective method of treatment as well – because it is an anticonvulsant. It's typically ingested in oil form, either on its own or mixed with food. The reason why CBD is so effective is because it easily interacts with the body's internal system.

Like humans, dogs have cannabinoid receptors throughout the central nervous system and in the brain. It's still a bit unclear as to how exactly CBD has become such an effective method of treatment. The general theory states that when CBD connects to these cannabinoid receptors, its natural anticonvulsant properties help restore normalcy to these abnormally firing neurons, thereby calming and relaxing your pup and preventing the onset of a seizure.

And, unlike some traditional medications for dogs, CBD oil has no life-threatening side effects when used in the proper dosage. It doesn't pose a risk to the kidneys, liver, or GI tract. Of course, as with any medication, there are risks, but overall CBD oil for dogs acts as a highly effective and more natural alternative to pharmaceutical methods.

How do you use CBD for dog seizures?

If you're unfamiliar with CBD and what to look for, a good place to start is checking for quality. Fortunately, you can find high-quality CBD in the form of oil, capsules, and dog treats. Once you've identified an appropriate form of CBD, check to see if it's organic and how it's been processed. High-quality CBD oils are made from organically grown hemp and are not processed. CBD oils also vary in bioavailability. You will want to find a product with high bioavailability. Canna-Pet products provide 10-15 times more bioavailability than traditionally digested products.

Now that you know more about the impact CBD oil can have on your dog's seizures, you may want to consider it as a primary method of treatment – especially for pups with recurring seizures or epilepsy. Given the effectiveness of CBD, it's no wonder more dog owners are giving it a try.

Use this guide as a reference, and of course, talk to your veterinarian with any questions you may have. Be sure that you fully understand all treatment options and are comfortable with your decision. You need to do what's best for both you and your dog in order to treat and prevent these seizures.

Benefits Of Cannabis Oil For Dogs

You should consider CBD oil while creating a daily wellness regimen for your dog's behavior training and proper healthy diet.

Several studies reported that CBD oil for dog significantly reduces pain and prevent inflammation and swelling.

It makes the dog feel incredibly relaxed, lessens anxiety issues, and helps in improving the quality of sleep. CBD oil extracted from hemp has numerous positive effects on the dog's health.

- It treats epilepsy and seizures and reduces the frequency of them. It reduces the activity of neurons and attacks free radicals preventing anxiety attack and seizures.

- CBD oil being a pain reliever causes a reduction in pain by targeting specific aching joints and relieving pain. Also, it prevents chronic inflammation in dogs suffering from arthritis and helps them in proper healing.

- Don't worry when your dog refuses to eat and loses its appetite because CBD oil helps in improving taste and alleviates all the digestive issues.

- Many dogs suffer depression and anxiety that leads to destructive behaviors like pacing and urinating anywhere. Anyhow, CBD oil is a relaxing stimulant and helps in relieving stress and calming your pet.

- It helps in reducing cancer symptoms in dogs by its anti-tumor properties. CBD oil kills the cancer cells in association with the immune system and blocks their activity, invasion, and spread.

- Long-term use of CBD oil helps in enhancing the systemic balance and reducing the stress.

- Overall it helps in treating various cardiovascular, neurogenerative, inflammatory bowel, and autoimmune diseases.

CBD Oil For Dog Seizures – How It Works?

Just like humans, practically all animals possess an endogenous cannabinoid system in their body. This endocannabinoid system plays a vital role in maintaining emotional balance and health, enhancing the healing process, and regulating the immune system.

The ECS consists of endocannabinoids that act on the neuroreceptors that control the production of several proteins and hormones.

CBD oil performs its function by targeting its corresponding receptors located in various organs, brain, immune cells, and central nervous system that assists in stimulating the relaxing effects.

CBD oil for dogs has proven to be as efficient as the traditional medical treatment for treating certain types of seizures.

Few studies attributed that CBD oil for dogs have been proved to reduce the inflammation associated with the seizures and regulates the neuronal activity.

The exact biological mechanism by which CBD oil helps in preventing seizures is still unknown; however, it works better than all the standard therapies used for seizures.

Just because CBD oil is a non-psychoactive stimulus, it provides calming sensations to your dog and efficiently helps in relieving pain without producing any potential intoxicating effects.

The production of free radicals in the body generates the oxidative stress and damage the dog's nervous system.

The CBD oil for dogs attacks the free radicals through its antioxidant property and serves as a natural remedy for treating dog's seizures. Thus, accurate CBD dosage for a dog is one of the potent treatments available.

What Research Says?

Most of the research performed to discover the effects of CBD oil on epilepsy or seizures have been conducted either on humans or lab animals such as cats and dogs.

Also, dogs possess an endocannabinoid system similar to the human, meaning they counter to cannabinoids in the same way as humans.

Thus, CBD is considered as a well-tolerated supplement for dogs as it helps in treating seizures and is completely non-toxic.

The American Epilepsy Society published a study confirming that CBD oil is effective in treating seizures. They tested the potency, safety, and efficacy of CBD oil on young adults and children suffering from severe types of epilepsy. The study found out that CBD reduces the frequency of these seizures by 45%. This study supported much research on animals and prior reports presenting that CBD can be a promising treatment for seizures.

Another study that was published in 2016, in a highly valued, peer-reviewed medical journal named The Lancet Neurology showed that CBD oil efficiently reduces the seizure attacks by an average of 36%.

They examined around 210 patients who had epilepsy for almost twelve weeks and treated them with 99% natural CBD extract. Also, they reported that nearly 2% of their patients got rid of their seizures entirely with the following treatment.

What Is The Accurate Dosage Of CBD Oil For Dogs?

To determine the perfect dosage of CBD oil for dogs, make sure to look for some factors that include your dog's breed, its health condition, history of the disease, weight or size of your dog, CBD oil concentration, delivery mechanism, and variances in the metabolism of your dog.

Starting with a lower dosage of CBD oil for dogs and increasing it gradually up to the required daily dose is an optimum measure. Notice the effects and adjust the amount of CBD oil accordingly. Ideally, the starting dosage of CBD oil for dogs should be as low as 0.05 mg of CBD/kg of your dog's body weight.

Administer three small doses of CBD to your dog over the course of the day instead of giving one significant dosage of CBD. Dogs weight ranging between 25 to 35 kg requires a daily dose of 9mg of CBD oil whereas dogs weighing more than 35 kilograms need a regular dose of 15 mg.

CBD oil dose can be handled unconventionally for dogs as it has no severe side effects or overdose limit. It is essential to your monitor your dog's health and behavior. Increase the CBD oil dose by 5 mg after every four to five days if you observe no improvement.

Administer 15mg of CBD oil daily from day 1 to 4. From day 5, increase it to 25 mg and ultimately after day 10, raise it over 35 mg if necessary. The overall period required for seizure treatment is 90 days.

Continue monitoring your dog's health and its symptoms and when you observe the signs are gone, keep on administering the same CBD dose for two more weeks for concluding the treatment correctly.

How To Administer CBD Oil To The Dogs?

There are various ways of administering CBD oil to your dog. Administer it sublingually under its tongue if you are not scared of its teeth. However, if your dog is not that trained, then you can apply a few drops of CBD oil on your hand and let the dog lick it.

If you are unable to adopt any of these ways, then you can mix drops of CBD oil with your dog's food or give it by mixing in drinking water.

The best way of administering CBD oil to your dog is sublingual application because it allows the cannabinoids and terpenes to come in close contact with the blood tissues present in the mouth. This method helps in absorbing CBD directly into the bloodstream.

The sublingual application delivers the therapeutic effects of CBD oil rapidly within 30 seconds to two minutes. Also, it is possible that 30 to 60% of your

CBD oil dosage gets vanished due to the lower bioavailability in the digestive tract and the acidic stomach acids.

Sublingual application using a dropper is the most accessible method to adopt because it helps in measuring the dose of CBD oil for dogs accurately.

Potential Risks Of CBD Oil On Dogs

Every other supplement has some side effects while the medical cannabis for dogs is okay. High-quality CBD oil for dogs contains zero-level or only trace amounts of THC, which is what makes your dog feels high.

Therefore, the most severe potential risk associated with CBD oil might be lethargy or drowsiness. Also, excess consumption of CBD oil has no long-term side effects.

CBD containing high THC strains can cause severe side effects or static ataxia in dogs, for this reason,

CBD oil with THC is firmly rejected by multiple veterinarians.

CBD oil is a non-toxic and non-psychoactive supplement that has beneficial effects on the dog's health. It does not interact with any other supplement or medication thus considered safe and efficient for treating various medical conditions in dogs.

Full spectrum CBD often contains terpenes that efficiently amplify the positive effects of CBD oil on dogs.

The most common potential risks associated with the non-psychoactive CBD oil include drooling, vomiting, dizziness, lethargy, unusual behavior, agitation, and depression.

Best CBD Oil For Dogs

Make sure to start your dog's CBD treatment with a high quality and lab tested CBD oil to avoid any potential risks and achieving the best results.

Also, visit your veterinarian and ask him to prescribe you the best CBD oil. However, just to make it easy for you, here is a list of some of the highest quality CBD oil available in the market.

- Get CBDPet –

Get CBDPet developed its CBD oil products for those who want to maximize their health and treat various diseases without any compromise. They provide natural and organic oil containing terpenes and other cannabinoids.

All of their products are quality tested and without any pesticides or chemicals. They further offer a 90-day money-back guarantee because customer satisfaction is their top priority.

- fxCBD

They are one of the best sellers of the CBD oil. They extract CBD oil from the highest quality hemp plants. Their initial aim is to provide the purest and cleanest CBD oil to their customers.

They mix CBD oil with amino acids, minerals, vitamins, and fatty acids, hence making it beneficial for both animals and humans.

It is free from all the chemicals and pesticides. It is entirely certified and is best for your pet because it provides all the health benefits that your dog deserves.

- PurCBD

CBD tinctures for dogs from PurCBD is advantageous because their CBD oil is also full spectrum and completely natural.

It is considered to be one of the best CBD oil by many veterinarians in the medical community as it is non-psychoactive and free of chemicals.

Also, their CBD oil is available at affordable prices. Their products get checked regularly after every extraction process for its potency, quality, cleanliness, and safety.

Verified Dog Treats of CBD

Many veterinarians prescribe CBD oil from Verified CBD because of their high standards of production and quality check.

They produce the purest CBD oil available in the market because they implement the recent technologies and strictly follows the GMP manufacturing guidelines.

People love CBD oil from verified CBD because of their quality, value for money, and product innovation.

Also, their products get tested after every production by HPLC equipment for checking the presence of any pesticide or chemical, microbiological contamination, and detecting the terpene profile.

CONCLUSION

Various cannabinoids including cannabidiol have significant effects on the health of human beings as well as on animals. As research on CBD oil persists to emerge, pet owners are exploring the fact that medical cannabis can impart beneficial effects for dogs.

Usually, pet owners feel devastated when they see their dogs suffering from any health problem like anxiety, pain, or seizures. However, CBD containing anti-seizure, anti-inflammatory, anxiolytic, and anti-psychoactive properties, has been proved useful for treating various health conditions and maintaining the health of animals.

Thus, pet owners are increasingly considering CBD oil for dogs with high levels of anxiety or have seizures.

In spite of the fact that there are numerous medicines available in the market that can be used for treating seizures or any other health problem, they cause multiple adverse side effects. However, one drug, in particular, that is discovered proficient by many veterinarians is cannabidiol. Administering CBD oil to your dog is a perfect remedy because it is 100% natural and healthy. Also, it is free of chemicals and other injurious substances. Means that CBD oil could treat your pet, avoiding the use of harmful drugs.

CPSIA information can be obtained
at www.ICGtesting.com
Printed in the USA
LVHW020310011222
734393LV00015B/1799

9 781654 865962